The Ultimate Waiter:
The 50 Quickest Ways To Make An Extra $100 In Tips This Week!

Robert McHalffey

Thank you so much for purchasing this book! Please take the time to go to Amazon.com and leave an honest review. Your opinion is important to me.

Introduction

I put off writing this manual for a long time. I always knew that the information in these pages was solid and useful, but I thought that the things I wanted to discuss were common sense among the serving community. However, after years of going out to eat in restaurants and watching my co-workers, it is apparent that these strategies are not necessarily taught to servers by the management staff.

These tips, tricks, and methods of going about things are not just theory. They are sound techniques that have been used not just by me, but also by my peers, time and time again. This way of doing things will undoubtedly increase guest satisfaction and check averages so that you, the server, end up getting tipped a higher percentage based on your now higher sales, which in turn leads to more money in your pocket.

An EXTRA $100 per week with 52 weeks a year yields an EXTRA $5,200 in your yearly income. What would you do with that extra cash? I know what I would do, but if I told you, you would probably return my book.

-Robert McHalffey

The Goods

The tips and tricks listed here in "The Goods" are designed to give you the quickest and best bang for your buck. These are things that you can begin doing **today** to <u>make more money</u>.

The section that follows this, "Serving: From Head to Toe," is more of a complete service manual for the less experienced waiter. However, all of the information in this book will help you increase your tips (even if you're a seasoned veteran), so let's get started!

1. Turn Your Tables

The time that a guest sits down until the time that they pay and leave is one "turn" of a table. Your goal is to have as many of those, in one night, as possible.

All other things being equal, if Server 1 turns her four table section five times (20 tables), while Server 2 only turns his four table section four times (16 tables), at the end of the night Server 1 has had 25% more guests than Server 2, which in turn leads to 25% more tips. Example: $75 vs. $100.

In order to aid in the turning of your tables, you can do a number of things. For instance, *pre-bussing your tables* (taking away plates, utensils, glassware, etc. that the guests are no longer using) so that when it is time for the busser to clean your table there is very minimal clean-up and they can therefore re-set and re-seat your table more quickly.

Also, make sure to *ring in food at appropriate times*. You never want to rush your guests, but you also don't want to have them sitting at your table for two hours when they could have been gone in an hour and a half. Find the balance.

2. Always Take That Last Table

It's the end of the night. You are probably going to get cut soon and you just want to go home. But...of course. Here comes one last table. Do you take it or give it to another server? I know you're tempted, but...

TAKE IT.

Money is money is money. You are already at work and you have no clue what this table will order or how much they will tip. Some of my best tips, tips that saved my entire night, have come from that last table.

3. Pick Up That Extra Shift

This tip is kind of a given, but people don't utilize it nearly enough. People will, without irony, in the same sentence, talk about how broke they are and how they didn't make any money tonight, and then ask if anyone can pick up their Friday night shift so that they can go to a party. There are always shifts to be picked up. Take advantage of that. Pick up that extra shift.

If you do only three things after reading this book and those three things are "Turn Your Tables," "Always Take That Last Table," and "Pick Up That Extra Shift," you will make an extra $100 per week, minimum, guaranteed.

Also, figure out which shifts make the most money. Ask your teammates how much they usually make on that day or this night. Then, if you are faced with the option of picking up one or the other, you can go with the more lucrative option.

4. Have A Minimum In Mind

Have you ever noticed that when rent or your car payment is due that you always seem to make just enough money in time to pay your bills? Always go into work knowing how much money you want/need to make that shift. Decide on a minimum and do not leave until you have made at least that much money.

5. Smile

This one is as simple as it gets, but people forget to do it all of the time. Listen, I get it. Sometimes life hands you lemons, your chips are down, the odds are stacked against you. But nobody likes a Debbie Downer and when I go into an establishment and I am paying good money for a product, or service, the last thing that I want is for the person helping me to make me feel like I am unwanted or unappreciated because they decided it's crappy-attitude-mopey-face day.

Bad attitudes don't get tips. SMILE ☺

6. Call Your Guest By Name

This is a cool, simple little trick, but it works wonders. If guests introduce themselves to you by name, remember it and then use it for the remainder of their visit.

"Jason, would you like another iced tea?"

"Bob. Phyllis. Enjoy the rest of your night. Feel free to come back and see me anytime."

"Nancy, please stop touching my ass."

This also helps to create regulars. Regulars are guests that come back to the restaurant time and time again simply to see YOU. They are usually great tippers and they come back all of the time. If you can create a good rotation of five to ten regulars that come back every month and tip big, then most of your income is guaranteed. I have a friend who got a $20,000 tip from her regulars in order to put her through college. Far fetched? Hard to believe, I know, but it happened once, it could always happen again.

7. Make Your Guests Laugh

This one may be harder than it sounds, because some people just aren't funny and some guests aren't going to laugh even if you're the next stand-up superstar. But, if you can get your guests to chuckle, laugh 'til they wet themselves, or pretty much anything in between, then you have them in the palm of your hand.

8. Relate To Your Guests

This means communication, folks. If you don't know where to start, try asking questions like:

"Are we celebrating anything special today?"

"I noticed your accent. If you don't mind me asking, where are you from?"

Or even as simple as...

"Did you catch the game today?"

Anything that will give you a chance to open up the lines of communication to the guest and to show them that you are a cool, fun, or likeable person. Not to mention that the more a guest likes and relates to you, the better chance you have of creating regulars.

9. Complimentary Samples

First and foremost, make sure that your management is OK with sampling. The last thing you want is to get fired over something as silly as giving away a taste of sauce. However, if management is fine with it (as they most likely will be), then sampling is a great way to build rapport with your guests. This can be used to allow them to compare soups, wine, beer, raspberry lemonade vs. regular lemonade, etc...

It's better to take the time to allow a guest to find out what something will taste like with a small sample than to have them order an entire portion of something that they might actually hate... and send back.

Samples. Do it.

10.   Be The Face Of Your Table

This is extremely important.

Even if your restaurant has food runners, liquor runners, and server assistants that do some of the tasks at your table for you (e.g. bringing out your food, drinks, grabbing the guests water, etc.), I recommend doing as much of these things yourself as possible so that YOU are the person that the guest sees the most. This goes back to creating a rapport with your guest, as well.

Obviously, sometimes these people are more necessary than at other times, due to the volume of the restaurant, but when things are slower and you can afford more face time with your guests, then I urge you to do so.

11.   Do 1% More Than Expected

This pretty much goes for everything that you do.

The guest will always have an expectation of what is going to happen and all you have to do is that little extra 1% and they will be "wow-ed." This will be different for every restaurant you work in based on the resources you have on hand.

For example, in a restaurant that I used to work at we had these little homemade cookies that we were allowed to offer guests for special occasions. If things didn't go as smoothly as possible at any particular table, one could say, "Folks, you have been extremely patient through this entire process. As a token of my appreciation and because things haven't gone as smoothly as I would have liked, I have brought out some homemade cookies for you to enjoy free of charge." The expectation, for the guest, is for everything to go smoothly or for you to fix whatever has gone wrong. They do not, however, expect that last little bit of hospitality, that extra 1% and that makes all the difference.

12.   Be Special

If there is something about your restaurant, or you, that is special... sell the sh%t out of it.

About 6 years ago when I was bartending in Cleveland, Ohio, I would make my own version of the alcoholic rum drink called the "zombie." My name is Rob and the drink was my twist on a "zombie" so I dubbed it the "Rob Zombie."

The best part about it is that it's a florescent blue tropical looking drink, so all I would have to do is make one and all of a sudden the entire bar was wondering what "that person" was drinking and before you knew it, the entire bar was filled with "Rob Zombies." It was my trademark and people came straight to me, and only me, for it. Be Special.

13. Anticipate The Guests' Needs

The best and most proactive way to do this is to make it an attainable goal. Try to set the goal that no guest will need to ask for anything because you will have already asked them if they need said thing or will have already grabbed it for them.

This just comes with practice and with paying attention. If someone orders French fries they will most likely want ketchup. If it's iced tea they will want lemon and sweetener, for pasta they will want Parmesan cheese, steak will need a steak knife, etc... This also goes for re-filling guests' beverages, boxing up their food, and bringing out a dessert menu. The list goes on and on.

YOU ARE THE EXPERT. You are the one that spends 30 hours a week in this restaurant with this food developing a system that works for you so that when a guest sits down at your table they will undoubtedly receive some of the best service that they have ever had. And they will tip you for it, and they will tell their friends, and they will come back and bring their friends and they will all tip you together. YAY!

14. Clicky Pens

This is just a fun little trick that I have picked up along the way that I have really liked and have stuck with it. The idea is that when you give a guest a "clicky" pen to sign their credit card slip, they will tip more than if you gave them a regular ballpoint pen. I'm not quite sure if this is just restaurant folklore or if there is some sort of actual behavioral science behind it, but I have been doing it now for about ten years and I'm never going back.

15.   Get a Manger Involved If Possible

Don't ever be the bad guy. If a guest wants something that your restaurant doesn't allow, or is against company policy, then get a manager involved. Regardless of how silly the guest's request is, there is no use in you trying to "teach them a lesson" or to take blame for something that you have no control over.

> Example: You drop off the check and the guest tries to pay you with multiple coupons.
>
> Guest: Here. We have these five coupons.
> Server: These coupons are limited to one per table. I'm sorry.
> Guest: Well, they let me use them last time I was here!
> Server: I understand, let me ask my manager and I'll be right back.

I realize that it's absurd for a guest to think that they can get a $100 discount because they have multiple coupons, but who cares? It's not your restaurant or your money, so smile and get a manager involved. This way you can protect what is yours: your tip.

16. Automatic Gratuity

If you can add automatic gratuity to a table, usually parties of 6 or more, then do it. I hear servers complain all of the time about getting "stiffed" on a check because they didn't add the gratuity, expecting to get tipped more than the "auto grat."

Don't gamble with your money. Add the gratuity and then when you drop off the check, say something to the guest like, "Our computer automatically adds gratuity to parties of 6 or more, but if you would like to leave more you are more than welcome."

If you did your job and they loved you, then they will tip more than the gratuity. Trust me.

17. Accept Responsibility For Your Actions

Honesty goes a long way. For example, if a guest asks you for butter and ten minutes later you realize that you forgot their butter, simply get the butter, take it to the table, and say something along the lines of "Folks, I'm such a doofus. The butter completely slipped my mind. Here it is. Sorry about that."

Yes, I just used the word "doofus" and I'm pretty sure there was a pun in there somewhere. Why?

Because that particular word doesn't offend anybody and it makes the guest laugh. They love corny sh%t like that. Obviously, you can come up with your own little apology, but the point is that there is no need to lie about butter. Just tell the truth, *sincerely* apologize, and walk away.

18.   Go Out To Eat

This may sound silly, but it is one of the best, although passive, ways to become a better server. It allows you to realize some of the things that bother you as a restaurant patron. It also gives you insight and ideas into what good service is and new ways to "wow" your own guests.

Serving: From Head to Toe

Looking Presentable

19. Clean and Press Your Clothes

Increasing your tips starts before your guests even step foot in the door. It starts with your uniform, which says something about you before you even have a chance to open your mouth. It is the guest's first impression of you, and as the old saying goes, you only get one chance to make a first impression (technically the cleanliness of your section is their first impression of you, but more on that later).

Now, uniform obviously changes depending upon your work environment, but the basics hold true regardless. Clothes should be clean and pressed. It doesn't matter whether I go to a fine dining restaurant, a local dive bar, or anything in between. I want the person who is touching my food and/or drinks to have an outfit that isn't covered in some sort of mystery sauce or looks like they pulled it out of their back seat after a long night of drinking.

20.   Well Kept Hair

Women, this means that if you are serving food your hair is placed in a ponytail or a bun. I realize that most of you think that your hair is far sexier down than it is when it's up. However, it only takes one fallen strand of hair in someone's pasta or your hair going into someone's martini when you lean over the table to drop off/pick something up, to take your tip from 20% to non-existent.

Men, this means that you always have some sort of product in your hair. None of that fluffy hair nonsense. I would also recommend that you get your hair cut on a regular basis or at least have a friend trim up the unsightly overgrown hair that accumulates at the bottom of your neck and sticks out from underneath your shirt. This is, of course, assuming you have short hair. Obviously, if you have long enough hair to pull back, then the same rule applies for the men as to the women. Pull your hair back into a ponytail. And if you work in a place that allows you to wear hats, and you want to wear one, then cool. Wear a hat... but trim your neck hair.

21.   Tidy Facial Hair

Hopefully, this only applies to the men, but just in case... Ladies, if you also have facial hair-- GET IT REMOVED. Nothing is more unappetizing than looking at the sweat accumulate on the mustache of the female waiter serving me my food. Men should either be clean-shaven or keep their facial hair tidy. Make sure it always looks as if whatever is going on with your face has been planned. If you are growing a beard, great, but trim the neck up. Make an effort. Don't let your facial hair look as though it's there on accident.

22. Non-Slip Shoes

How can non-slip shoes increase your tips, you ask? They allow you to move/work harder and faster in areas like the kitchen, behind the bar, and anywhere else that has a slippery, wet, greasy surface. This increased productivity allows you to do everything that you need to do for your guests in a more productive/efficient manner.

This increased productivity allows you to turn your tables (see #1) more quickly, which will account for more sales and more money in your pocket. And with all of the options and styles we have now-a-days for non-slip shoes (they even make Converse style non-slips) there is no reason not to wear them.

23. Clean Your Fingernails

Men, clean and trim your fingernails. Ladies, the same goes for you. If you have painted nails, definitely keep them looking nice. It does not do you any good to have the chipped, cracked nails that some girls sport all too often. The guest looks at your hands more than you think.

Set Your Section Up for Success

24.   Make Your Section Clean

When you arrive at work, take a good look at your section. Your section, just like your uniform, says a lot about you as a server. As a matter of fact, people will see your section before they ever see you.

If I sit down at a place to eat and the table is dirty, the glassware is dirty, and the floor is not swept, I am most likely not going to think very highly about the server who's working that station. Whether it is the bar top for bartenders or your tables for servers, you need to make sure that your section is clean.

This means that the floors around your area need to be swept, the counters or tabletops need to be clean and reset, any silverware and glassware to be placed on the tables need to be clean and polished (no watermarks, residue, lipstick marks, etc.).

You are the owner of your section; it is your own small business for the night. It is the vehicle by which you will pay your bills and fund your life, so RUN IT LIKE YOU OWN IT.

25.   Stock Yourself Up

There is usually an area near your section that holds all of your back-up items: plates, silverware, glassware, condiments, lemons, olives, iced tea, lemonade, etc... Make sure that this area is fully stocked. It is a huge burden to realize in the middle of a busy shift that you need to cut more lemons or to run all the way in the back to grab ketchup. It is far easier to have all of these things near you so that can focus on more important things, like anticipating the guest's needs.

The Guest

26.   Greet The Table Within 30 Seconds

This allows enough time for them to get settled in, but not enough time for them to start wondering if they will be helped. Even if you only have time to walk by the table for a second, make sure that you make eye contact with the guest and tell them something simple like, "I'll be with you in one moment, folks." This will usually buy you a couple of minutes if you are busy so that the guests don't get antsy. The eye contact is key. If their heads are down and buried in the menu, they probably didn't hear you.

27. Don't Take It Personally

Be patient. Remember that when guests come into a restaurant, they are hungry. Hunger increases irritability and agitation. Add on top of that the bad day that they have had at work, the screaming kids on the car ride to the restaurant, and the fact that they are eating with their in-laws (whom they hate), and you have a pretty stressed guest.

Now, obviously not all guests are irritable and annoying. The point I'm trying to make is that if you come across one, don't take anything they say personally. They don't know you and they have barely even met you, so nothing they can say should have any bearing on how you feel.

28. Feed The Kids First

Children are DICTATORS. If they decide it's time to leave, it's time to leave. That's why guests that have small children, babies, or toddlers, are usually in a hurry. Children can only sit in one place for a small period of time. Make sure to immediately ask the appropriate questions:

Do you need a booster seat or high chair?

Shall I grab the kids something to drink right away?

Would you like me to get the children's food started first or is it OK if their meals come out with the rest of the food?

Do you need a muzzle for your screaming child?

The biggest tips come from grateful parents whose lives have been made easier because of an expedient server. Feed the kids first.

Beverages

29.   Add a Beverage

When taking the beverage order, it is always better to give the guest two specific options to choose from as opposed to asking a general question like, "Can I get you something to drink?"

Always offer two non-alcoholic drinks and two alcoholic drinks, preferably one cocktail and one wine. "May I start you off with a Raspberry Lemonade or an Iced Tea, perhaps a Pomegranate Martini or a glass of our house red wine?" This gives your guests clear visuals and options to chose from. It also gets them thinking about ordering things they might not have been thinking about ordering otherwise.

If you add one beverage (alcoholic or otherwise) per person to a four top of guests, on average that's about $5 per guest. That's an extra $20 per table, which accounts for about $4 in extra tips. Multiply that by the 10 tables you have in a night and you're looking at an extra $40 for that night alone.

30.   Up-Selling Beverages

Know your beverage menu. What beers do you have on tap versus in a bottle? Which liquors do you serve? Which glasses of wine do you have by the glass versus by the bottle?

This is important, because if a guest orders something general like a gin and tonic, you can immediately say, "Great. Would you prefer Hendricks, Tanqueray..."

Notice that I left the sentence open ended. It does not need to be finished. They will either choose one of the two options that you gave them, ask if you have another brand besides those two, or they will choose to go with the house (house or well means the cheapest version of that specific liquor that your bar carries). This method can be used for any other drink, whether they ask for a Vodka Martini, Whiskey Sour, Rum and Coke, etc...

You should also know which specialty drinks can be up-sold. Long Islands, for example, can be ordered regular or top-shelf. Top Shelf is the more expensive version of this drink. Instead of using well liquor it's made with your top-shelf liquor like Grey Goose, Bacardi, Tanqueray, and Grand Marnier.

31. Refills

Make sure that you are bringing a refill of the guest's beverage IN A FRESH GLASS when their current beverage is about half empty. This allows you enough time to return to the table with their drink before they have finished their current one.

I emphasize "in a fresh glass" particularly because of iced tea. People like their iced tea a very particular way (i.e. two Splenda's, one sugar, four equals, etc.) and if they spend their time making their iced tea perfect and you come over, when their glass is half empty, with a pitcher of iced tea, and mess with their ratio, they will not be thrilled.

In a nationwide study regarding what people thought made good service at a restaurant, "Drink Refills" was listed as number one. Think about it.

32. Refilling Water

The exception to the Fresh Glass Rule is water. Take note, if you are bringing a pitcher of water to the table for refills, do yourself a favor and remove the glass from the table while you top it off. It is far too easy to accidentally pour water onto someone's cell phone/wallet/ipad/lap or to accidently knock something over. Take the extra two seconds and remove the glass from the table while refilling it.

33.   Alcoholic Beverage Refills

The same thing applies for alcohol as it does for soda. If the glass is half empty, ask if they would like another. However, it is especially important to ask the guest right before their entrées come to the table. Something like...

"Your entrées will be out in a couple of minutes. Would you like me to get you another Pinot Noir/Sam Adams/Lemon Drop Martini so that you can enjoy it with your meal?"

This will get them to order another alcoholic beverage about 80% of the time.

Upselling Is an Art

34.   Always An Opportunity

The goal of up-selling is to always be up-selling. Do not feel bad about doing this. You are simply giving the guests options that they might not have known they had. The guests are out on the town, they are treating themselves to a nice meal that is prepared by someone else. They *want* to be wined and dined and to have the fullest experience that your establishment has to offer. It is therefore your job to give them extraordinary options.

This is, of course, not a license to be pushy. You are simply informing the guest of the great and special things that your restaurant has to offer and the benefits of these choices. The choice is up to them. Don't be discouraged if, after all of your grand up-selling, they choose to go with something as simple as water. Even then there is the opportunity for a friendly, "Perfect. I can get you a bottle of Panna, Pellegrino, or simply tap water."

35.   Verbally Reward Your Guest

I have noticed that I feel really good about my server when they make me feel happy about my decisions, especially when I have taken the more economic route. When your guest orders, you can reply with "Great," "Perfect," or "Wonderful." People like to be complimented, so compliment away.

36.   Only Sell Good Food

If there is an item, or items, on the menu that you genuinely dislike, or that people constantly send back, let the customer know. For example:

Customer: We'll have the onion strings for an appetizer.

Server: Have you had the onion strings before?

Customer: No, are they good?

Server: I think they work great as a garnish, but they aren't my favorite appetizer. However, all of our other appetizers are amazing. I recommend the Thai Lettuce Wraps with our made-to-order soy sauce. They're amazing.

Customer: Well, thank you so much, we'll take the Lettuce Wraps then.

You might as well get the guest something that they are going to love on the first try. This will save you time and now you're not stuck with the task of having the chef re-make something while the guest sits there without food (and everyone else at the table eats). Of course, if the guest has already had this item in the past and they liked it, simply allow them to order it again.

It's All In The Timing

37. Drinks To The Table Within Two Minutes

After the guest has placed their drink order, be sure to return with said drinks within two minutes. If the drinks are going to take a little bit longer (e.g. the bartender is in the weeds, the beer keg needs changing, liquor/wine needs to be grabbed from the back, etc.), simply drop off a couple glasses of ice water and inform the guest of the situation.

People usually don't mind waiting as long as they are kept "in the loop" about the process and why it's taking longer than usual. For example:

> Server: Hey folks, the bartender is changing the keg for your Sam Adams. Here are a couple of glasses of water while you wait. If you like, I can go ahead and take your appetizer/entrée order so that we can get the kitchen started on your food while we wait for the drinks.

This stops a situation from ever arising regarding the wait time on cocktails. You give them the water to quench their thirst and to show them that you have not forgotten about them. You get their food working so that the kitchen can begin cooking your guests' food while you simultaneously wait for drinks at the bar or handle the guests at other tables.

38. Many Hands Make Light Work

Don't be afraid to ask for help when you need it! If you cannot get to a table quickly enough, or you are too busy to grab the guests' drinks from the bar, or you need someone to check on the food in the kitchen... ASK FOR HELP! Grab anyone who looks like they are LESS BUSY than you. Your teammates should be more than happy to help you and this way the guest doesn't suffer.

Also, always know what can be done to help you. If a fellow teammate sees that you are busy and wants to help, you should know exactly what can be done in order for them to make your life easier at that moment in time. Example:

Server 1: Do you need help with anything?

Server 2: Yes! Can you please box up the food for table two and grab a Sprite for table 21?

Server 1: Of course!

See, because you knew exactly what needed to be done in order to make your life easier, your life is easier.

Knowledge Is Power

39. Know Your Menu!

In order to sell the food in your restaurant in the most effective and efficient manner you must first know your menu. This means specials, entrées, appetizers, soups, salad, desserts, cocktails, wines, liquor, beers, ports, EVERYTHING! If it's on the menu then know it. You are the expert and the guest should feel as if they are in good hands while dining at your table. This will also allow you to do two things.

1.) Answer any and all questions that arise without the need to ask someone else, which would in turn slow down the speed of service and therefore increase the amount of time that tables are sitting in your section.
2.) It will allow you to suggestively up-sell items in order to increase your check average.

"Sir you ordered the filet mignon. I recommend making that dish a surf and turf item by adding a lobster tail."

"Would you like to add [insert protein item here] to your pasta/salad?"

40. Give Personal Endorsements

When up-selling, it is always more effective to give personal endorsements. Guests are more inclined to purchase something if they think that it is your personal favorite or "the most popular choice among guests" or "hands down the best item on the menu."

41. No Sticker Shock

"Sticker Shock" is when you get a bill for something and it's much higher than you anticipated due to "hidden" fees. Make sure to inform the guests of any additional costs that will be incurred due to their choices.

Guest: May I add shrimp to my pasta?

Server: Absolutely. There will be a slight upcharge of $4.00. Will that be OK?

Guest: Yes, that's fine. Thanks for asking!

Guests do not like sticker shock. If you word something incorrectly and they think that the $4.00 soup or salad that they just ordered comes with the meal, at no additional charge, they will most likely blame you for not making it clear to them. This usually ends in them taking it out of your tip or complaining to management. Either scenario blows. (Pardon my French)

The Main Dish

42. Don't Overlap Food Courses

When a guest orders both appetizers and entrées it is important that they will have enough time to enjoy their appetizer/soup/salad before the entrées hit the table. Your goal should be to have the entrées hit the table about 3 minutes after they have finished their appetizer (first course) and you have cleared the table for their entrées (second course).

This will vary depending on how busy the kitchen is at that moment and the food item that was ordered.

The best way to handle this will be to communicate with the chef, the coordinator, or the expeditor (expo), and to *know your menu*. If your chef tells you that ticket times are running long and you know that the guest's Veal Porterhouse Steak will take 35 minutes to cook, then you should ring in the steak immediately after you ring in the calamari. On the other hand, if it's not a busy shift and the kitchen is running smoothly, then you should probably wait until the crab cakes appetizer has hit the table before you ring in the guest's entrée that you know will take no longer than 6 minutes to prepare. It's all about communication. Talk to your chef and know your menu.

43.   Split Their Food

If two guests tell you that they are sharing an item, talk to the kitchen and see if they will split the item onto two plates to make it easier for the guests. If the kitchen does not do this then make sure that when that food hits the table, there are plates ready for sharing.

If you have the time and would like to go a step further, you can always physically split the food up for the guests (actually serve the food at the table) onto their plates so that they do not have to fumble around with their pasta, chicken, etc.

44.   Check on Food Immediately

When any food hits the table it is customary to check on the table within two minutes or after they have taken two bites, whichever comes first. This is to make sure that everything has arrived at the table, has arrived correctly, tastes great, and that the guest does not require anything to accompany their dish (e.g. extra sauce, salt, pepper, utensils, etc.).

Personally, I like to instead check on the guest immediately and say something along the lines of "Hey folks, I just wanted to make sure everything came out alright." And if everything looks in order then I finish up with "I'll check back in a couple of minutes to make sure that it tastes amazing."

45.   Box Up The Guests' Food

Offer to box up the guests' food for them. It is far easier for you, the server, to do it than it is for the guest to fumble around at the table and perhaps accidentally pour sauce all over themselves in the process. Besides, this is an excellent "Step of Service" and it allows you the chance to go above and beyond their expectations. Even if your restaurant does not allow you to take it back to the kitchen, this can still be done at the table.

I also recommend writing on their to-go box. It can be just the basics, like the name of the food item in that box, the day, and the date. This helps them, when they have food sitting in the refrigerator at home, to identify what's in the box and whether or not it has been too long to enjoy it. Of course, if they insist on boxing it up themselves, simply bring the boxes and pre-bus the table to make it easier for them.

There Is Always Room For Dessert

46.   Always Room For Dessert

Dessert is one area in which servers severely lack up-selling skills. It is not enough to simply go up to a table and ask if they would like dessert. The answer to that question will most likely be "no" because people, in general, don't like to seem over-indulgent. Moreover, the server usually offers dessert with the expectation that the guests will say no. Remember that they are treating themselves. This could be the guests' one night out a month! Allow them to indulge by saying something like,

"Because I believe that no meal is complete without a delicious piece of cheesecake, I have brought over a dessert menu. Is it OK if I describe the desserts to you?"

Guests will rarely deny you the chance to describe the desserts once you ask permission. These descriptions, due to your amazing selling abilities (wink), will then trigger their senses. They are now far more likely to order a dessert than they would have been if you stuck to the "You guys want any dessert?" pitch.

47. After Dinner Drinks

These can be, but are not limited to: coffee, mocha, latte, cappuccino, espresso, hot tea, and ports. Get creative. Perhaps a guest doesn't want a dessert, but they would love a chocolate martini with a shot of Chambord in it ("Chocolate Covered Raspberry"). If you sell a $9 martini to a table, that's a $2 tip. If you do that to 10 tables, that's an extra $20 in your pocket. Money is money is money and it all adds up, so sell those after dinner drinks!

Time To Get Paid

48. Preview The Check

Be sure to preview the guest's check to make sure that it is correct and that you did not accidently add or omit something from their bill. Do not fall into the bad habit of "hooking people up" with free things unless, of course, management approves it. The major consequences (termination) far exceed the minimal perceived benefits (an extra dollar or two in tip). The majority of the time all that happens is the guest then tips you 25% on their now lower $40 bill ($10) when they would have tipped you 20% on their original $50 bill ($10).

49.   Run The Payment

When the guest is finished and ready to pay up, be sure to drop off the check and complete the payment process as quickly as possible. This is important for both you and the guest. You need the guest to leave so that the table can be turned (Turned = cleaned and sat with new guests) and so that they get can get to wherever they need to be (e.g. catch a movie, pick up the kids, get back to work, etc.).

50.   On The Subject of Change

If a guest pays cash, never ask if they need change. Simply say, "I'll be right back with your change." This allows them to stop you from getting change if it's unnecessary and it saves you from appearing needy, tacky, rude, and presumptuous.

In Conclusion

That's it folks! The 50 quickest ways to make an extra $100 in tips this week. Follow the advice outlined in this book and you will not only MAKE MORE MONEY but you will impress your management staff while doing it. Go out there and get 'em tiger!

Thank you so much for purchasing this book! Please take the time to go to Amazon.com and leave an honest review. Your opinion is important to me.

ABOUT THE AUTHOR

Robert McHalffey is from Cleveland, Ohio, but currently lives in Los Angeles, California. He has been working in the restaurant industry since 2001 and in his spare time enjoys acting, screenwriting, directing, and performing stand-up comedy. If you wish to contact him you can do so at R.mchalffey@gmail.com

www.ingramcontent.com/pod-product-compliance
Lightning Source LLC
Chambersburg PA
CBHW071550170526
45166CB00004B/1611